DEPRESSION BE GONE!

AF768903

Alyce Bartholomew Soden

Cover: "Rays of Hope"
by Penny Dreyer, Photographer
P.O. Box 44, Gualala, CA 95445 (707) 785-3580
Cover photo taken at The Sea Ranch, California

Library of Congress Catalog Number 95-71706

ISBN Number 0-9705329-1-1

Fish Rock Publishing Company
33801 So Hwy 1, Gualala, CA 95445-9515
(707) 884-3631 FAX (707) 884-3630

Printed By
CRS
Complete Reproduction Service, Inc.

Manufactured in the United States of America
96 95 94 93 92 10 9 8 7 6 5 4 3 2 1

Contents

I dedicate this book to my dear husband Jim. Without his loving support it would not be.

– A.S.

Chapter 1

DEPRESSION BE GONE!

Are you tired enough of this depression to say DEPRESSION BE GONE! Are you so thoroughly and physically sick and tired of being depressed all of the time to do something about it? Are you tired of putting off living, loving, working or anything else you have been putting aside until you are well enough to do it? Are you sick and tired of depression?

If you are, are you ready to try something new? You don't have to go anywhere, do anything different, spend any money. All you have to do is change your mind. That's not easy, you may say. You are right. It isn't easy. But you can do it.

Job 22:28 "You shall also decree a thing, and it will be established for you; And light will shine on your ways."

"I'm so depressed!" Do you ever hear yourself say these words? If you do you are decreeing more of the same. A decree knows not bad or good. It originates in your thought, comes out of your mouth and is set into motion by its own energy. You could just as well have said, "I'm so happy!" Then reasons to bring that about would be instigated in your inner belief and your outer world.

Listen to yourself. Sometimes your words reveal the space you are in, what you are thinking or have thought. Often these words jump out when you least expect them to reveal your mental and emotional level. Pay attention particularly when they are negative.

You have the power to choose exactly what you will say and think, and, as a result, bring this experience into your life. Decreeing a thing brings it forthwith into your life unless you immediately censor it. Job (in the Biblical account) in his time of depression and loss learned to charge his words with positive energy by decreeing the greatest good he could envision, and indeed a light did shine on his way. All that was taken from him was returned.

Now, I'm not saying this happened in the twinkling of an eye. It evidently took some time. He had to watch his words with great diligence while the action of his decree could be set into motion. Perseverance is the key.

Our words are a reflection of our thoughts. What thoughts do you entertain over and over on a regular basis? Someone dear is about to leave this life. Your job is being eliminated. Something is wrong with that project you started and have given your all to for a long time. Our thoughts run over and over sometimes seeking answers, but certainly affirming a negative fear. Instead of seeking the 'why' or the 'what' or the 'how', stop in mid thought and affirm something like

GOD IS ALWAYS DIRECTING ME TO MY HIGHEST AND GREATEST GOOD.

Stop that negative train of thought or it will manifest negative events in your life.

Depression is caused mainly by allowing our thoughts to run away into negativity over and over without stopping them. The most permanent method of controlling them is to consciously stop in mid-thought, examine its content and change it to the positive.

You may say, "My problem is getting up in the morning. I reach out, but just can't move."

My question is "What were you thinking when you went to sleep? Were they thoughts of great and wonderful plans for the morrow? Do you plan great and wonderful, exciting activities every day?

"Well, you may say, "I'm retired" or I'm on disability" so I don't go to work."

I say, "Plan great and exciting activities every day. Keep on living! Make every day an adventure. You can do it. Only you can do it".

Modern medicine has treated depression with mind-altering drugs of all kinds, but when the patients stop taking the drug; they return to the reality that their minds have set into motion. Their world hasn't changed much and / or their problems have grown to gigantic proportions while they were on the drugs. Even the best drug is not the solution.

Changing your mind, monitoring your thoughts, and replacing the negative with positive as soon as you recognize the pattern is the best suggestion I have. When you change your mind or thought, you also change the pattern that instigates your words.

Even happenstance words will reflect a change in your attitude and will bring about a change in your world. Escaping this life is no solution. Self-discipline is the answer. Consciously changing the pattern of your thought will change your world.

These words from an old song come to me:

> "I used to walk in the shade,
> With my blues on parade."

This is an apt definition of a person overwhelmed in depression. And this person may feel there is no way out while all the time they hold the key. CHANGE YOUR MIND! or Walk "on the sunny side of the street." as the song goes on. This is your choice: stay in depression or move into the light.

AFFIRM: DEPRESSION BE GONE!
I AM WALKING IN THE LIGHT, TODAY!

This powerful affirmation when used on a regular basis (said over and over when depressing thoughts come into your mind) contains the power to decree a new point of view. You can use it for your benefit.

What is the cause of depression? As much as we'd like to think, it is not what's happening to us in the world out there, but what we're allowing our thoughts to dwell upon inside us and our reaction to it, what we are giving our thought to about our life situation. Anyone's thought allowed to run away on a negative train will bring about depression. You are not alone. You can change it consciously by putting happy, positive, good thoughts in place of the depressing, hurtful thoughts. This seems too simple. Yes, it does, but it works! Start today to prove it to yourself. Make a plan and stick to it. You can heal yourself. Start the day decreeing:

DEPRESSION BE GONE! I AM WALKING IN THE LIGHT, TODAY!

Notes

Chapter 2

CAUSE OF DEPRESSION

So you're depressed, you say. What else is new? You've been this way for a long time. "Mind you, I have good reason to be depressed, what with Harvey passing after a long bout with cancer," or whatever your excuse is. Do you say this to yourself often?

You seem to be getting over it when along comes another tidal wave from life. Maybe the holidays trigger it, or a person you meet brings back memories or something unknown on your inner level.

Within yourself, you do know the cause. Sometimes it is helpful to bring the cause to your conscious mind. Simple exercises in revealing the subconscious mind are helpful:

1. Ask yourself this question as you drop off to sleep: Know that the answer will be revealed at that time or in the morning. What causes me to be depressed all the time? Record the answer that comes.

2. A journal may reveal your thought pattern. Analyze your journal according, to the time of year, activities, age, certain persons influence. Record you findings as the cause.

3. Document your thought pattern for a few days by setting a kitchen timer. When it goes off, write what you have been thinking for the previous hour. At the end of three days, evaluate the pattern of your thought. It many reveal the cause.

GREAT EXPECTATIONS

Depression can be caused by disappointment in yourself or another. We can become depressed when we know that we are not living up to some inner expectation. While growing up we tend to make heroes or look up to people we meet in the world. We try to emulate them. When we are not living up to that or some other preconceived idea, we can feel less than our greatest selves. People can go through a whole lifetime never realizing why they are so depressed.

When we turn 40 or 50 or any other time of passage, we are often reminded of what we set out to do, be or have in this lifetime. Often this triggers pictures in the subconscious mind of inner expectations which bring on depression. If you've failed your great expectations, knowing you are not desiring to increase that inner disappointment, is there some part of one of these expectations that you could still pursue? Perhaps you had planned to get a college education or take up knitting or learn to fly an airplane or some other special thing that you've always desired to do. It is not too late. You can do it, now! Well, you may say I can't because ______________________________ then sort through those great expectations until you, find one that you can do. Then say I can do this __________________________ _________________ now.

DO IT! Start right away, today.

Contracts with the Universe (God) not acted upon will bring about a depression that takes many strange and seemingly unrelated turns. A youngster was inducted into the priesthood of a church at the young age of fourteen. As he lived in this world, he succumbed to taking an alcoholic drink and felt that he was flawed and no longer eligible to hold that high honor. He continued to drink and became an alcoholic. For many years he lived this depressed sort of life. When he was fifty years old he woke up from his nightmare and, seeing what his life had become, he attended his first AA meeting. Gradually, he is rebuilding his life with honor.

Commitments made at an early age hold great power over our lives. The disappointment of not having lived up to our commitment can cause a lifetime of depression that may seem permanent. It is not a permanent situation and can be remedied.

Think back. Within you is a memory of your contract with God. Did you fulfill it? If not write it here on these lines.

Which part can you still accomplish? Write it here:

Set about doing it immediately.

You will be delighted how your depression will lift as you move toward fulfilling your God Contract.

Many people have had less than ideal upbringing in alcoholic, drug-ridden or abusive homes. Some have been molested or otherwise taken advantage of in life. These have caused the shadow of depression to obscure their vision of life and of themselves, and brings suspicion of others. Still throughout all this, the choice is still there. Take the advice of Job," Forgetting the past, I press on."

When we feel flawed by our own acts or another's action, it can cause a depression that continues throughout life. The only permanent remedy is to release that feeling of being less than good, to forgive ourselves or any others involved, and to discover who and what you are. You are not permanently scared by any action of another or yourself.

There is a spark within you that is untarnished by the events of life. Return to that inner spark and be renewed in Spirit. You can still be the greatest self you started out to be. Is it like an aching of the conscience? Far greater. It's like an aching of the soul that will not be satisfied by diversions of alcohol, drugs, sex or power over others. The aching of the soul is not satisfied until we return to our Spiritual Path.

As a nation we are now experiencing the effects of our aching souls. Many persons are lacking a conscience level of right and wrong and cannot evade the ache of the soul. Nothing satisfies until we return to God Consciousness.

Man is on a journey from God to God. There is no time limit. But progress in this area must keep up with our technology, or we are lost. All the technological advances we have made are as nothing if we do not develop the moral and ethical conscience to accompany them.

Our moral and ethical strength is our individual gift to the whole. As we exhibit an understanding of the highest and the best, and act as if it is so in our lives, it affects others in our vicinity. Before long the whole world is affected.

WHO'S FAULT IS IT?

It is easy to blame another, the world or luck for causing that miserable experience that happened to you. How could this happen to such a good person like yourself? You always want good things to happen to others and yourself included. It is not easy to accept the responsibility for setting this hurtful experience into motion on any level. You may say, "What? I didn't even contemplate this matter in any way!" There is no fault, and taking responsibility clears the way to rise above the matter, out of guilt and self-recrimination or blaming others into the space of looking for the good that will be brought about as a result of this.

Did you change your direction as a result of this trauma? It may well be that a greater good is in store for you than your direction was previously allowing. We seek to live the great and grand life. We do not know if it is painful when a lizard sheds his skin in order to grow. But often times when we grow the most, we experience great pain.

Release the self-defeating mechanism that is limiting you by seeking to find someone to blame; it's a waste of time and will create further problems of like nature. Let go of the hurts, fears, frustrations and pain and let God heal you. Make a space, search for the blessing, allow the Healing Presence to bring you back to balance. Start at the innermost, part of you, and let yourself heal. It was **NO ONE'S FAULT.** When you stop kicking yourself and others and let it rest, you will begin to heal.

If you are depressed, you affect someone near you. It has been my experience that if you involve your loved ones too much, they take on your burden, and when you least expect, it will be echoed back to you. It is your responsibility to heal yourself! No one else can do it for you. Others can encourage you, prescribe drugs, give you counseling and so on, but you have to change your mind.

Say over and over until you believe that it's true: **I AM HEALED OF ALL DEPRESSION, NOW! I CHOOSE TO BE FREE OF ALL VESTIGES OF THE BELIEF THAT I CAN EVER BE DEPRESSED.**

WHY NOT BLAME THE WEATHER FOR YOUR DEPRESSION?

Why not? That's as safe as anything else. Studies have shone that a lack of sunlight does affect us in many important ways, and depression is often the result. What is the answer? Get busy. Get totally involved in a project that demands your complete attention.

You may have discovered that you need more involvement with people at this time. So, expand your social calendar to include more happy and congenial people. Some of us tend to become moles instead of getting out into the light of friendship and laughter. Plan to laugh a lot.

If you are the social planner for your family, and if you or others in your family are susceptible to depression or getting cabin fever, which can take many forms, plan ahead. Get out, go to the movies. Have friends over. Fill up you calendar with play activities. Each one of these may not seem like much by themselves, but this is great preventive medicine. Try it You'll like it.

Depression, it appears to me, is the result of too much introspection, a belief that what we see in our conscious mind and without in our world is the true reality, which is just an appearance. It is the result of giving away one's Power to this deception.

Say **'NO MORE!" to depression!** Say **NO THANKS** to that little limited self who is always crying
(Depression may be identified as inner crying.)

Say **"YES" TO THE GOD SELF.** Look again with eyes to see your greatest self unfolding always in God's Light.

Every person has the potential to be depressed or exhilarated at any given moment. It depends on your choice.

What do you choose to be? Depressed or exhilarated? You may say, "That sounds so easy." Actually all it takes is a moderate amount of determination and a sincere desire to stick to it. You can do it! You can allow your mind to dissect your inner and outer world with a negative, tearing-down view, or you can just as easily build YOURSELF UP and FILL your world with a JOYOUS positive view.

Our minds work as a train running on a track if allowed to do so. The direction, content and quality of our mental life is always a result of our choice. All we have to do is change our thought about any given thing including ourselves and our life and experience both will change. We are not stuck in a tunnel with no choice even though it may appear to be so. Choose to come out of that tunnel and see the Light (good) more and more each day. Allow yourself to be that Light (good) by choosing light instead of darkness, exhilaration instead of depression. You can do it!

Affirm:
DEPRESSION BE GONE!
I AM WALKING IN THE LIGHT, TODAY, TOMORROW, EVERY DAY.

Notes

Chapter 3

FAKE IT UNTIL YOU MAKE IT

Do you have a friend or acquaintance who is so cheerful when you call that you dread calling? It is almost TOO painful . If you are aware of the contrast in attitude, it should indicate that you need to do some work on yourself. Don't give up that friend or rationalize that that person's attitude about life isn't realistic. Start finding ways to imitate your friend. Find ways to be cheerful even if you have to fake it. You know that if you practice a thing long enough you will become proficient at it. So, FAKE IT UNTIL YOU MAKE IT. Use your friend as a measurement of how your are progressing on your plan to fake it until you make it. Notice when it becomes not so painful to talk with your friend. Don't try to bring him down to your level. You step up to his.

I suggest that you start with a simple automatic action that you do all the time, such as putting on your glasses or picking up your pencil. Make a conscious effort to put on a happy face every time you do this action. Imprint these two plans into your consciousness until they become automatic. More and more you will discover that cheer-fulness is a habit that you can consciously cultivate.

It is my custom to inquire of my students when they call me, "What's the good word with you, today?" I have heard quite a variety of responses.

Usually, there is a long pause while the person reorganizes his thinking to the positive away from the negative problem facing him at that time.

A lady used to call me quite frequently. When I'd ask her "What the good word with her today was, the long pause was even longer. "I can't think of any good words today. It's a miserable day. It's been raining for a week and I can't work" Was her reply. I know my cheerful attitude really galled her. All efforts to turn her vision around seemed to be wasted. She was determined to stay in that negative rut of depression. You may have experienced this, also. Thank God it doesn't have to be permanent. It can be changed and you can do it. It is true, you do have to want to change before it will become a reality.

Cheerfulness is revealed in your words and actions as well as your happy face. Practice saying things of a positive nature and doing things that support your new change in plan. It is a plan. It has to be a conscious plan on all fronts, face, words, thoughts and deeds. Nothing else will do. Practice saying positive statements as I do. "What's the good word' has caused a change in the feeling and direction of the conversation on many occasions.

One of my more precocious students answered frequently, "Gods in His Heaven, and all's right with my world." or "God is all there is and I am a part of that All ness."

What happens when you consciously change your attitude? Your thoughts begin to change. You find it easier to think a cheerful thought. Create a vacuum by changing your depressed thoughts. Clean house, so to speak. Begin speaking from a happy, joyful point of view. Wouldn't it be better to have your mind focused on positive ideas rather than dwelling any longer on the negative? Negative and depressed thoughts are non-productive and limiting. They create a circle of endless results. It isn't long before you are experiencing what you set into motion. Therefore, it is in your best interest to pay attention and control your conscious thought. I have heard it asked," Do I want to spend my day with that thought, person or situation?" Dismiss it!

The vacuum you create by eliminating your depressed thought makes a space for something else that must be filled. This is automatic. Fill it with beauty, love, peace of mind, and prosperity. A positive affirmation that is useful is: **I am a happy, well adjusted, joyous person.** Millions of people have proved this Law to be true and have reprogrammed their lives by using it.

BIG GIRLS DON'T CRY

You have finally cried all your tears about this situation, beat yourself up with guilt or embarrassment. The time to stop is now! There is nothing you can do about the situation. It is time to forgive yourself and all others involved and get on with your life.

Stop a moment and look around at your life. Is it the way you want your life to be? Is it satisfying to your inner self? If it is not, you need to reinforce your foundation. Go back to your Center. Discover who and what you are and what you want your life to be like.

Isn't it wonderful that even though we may have gotten completely off course, we can always return to the Source and start out anew?

To me, long term depression is inner crying. You may have stopped crying on the outer, but the inner crying continues as a form of depression.

A lady shared with me: "I have an important decision to make. I'm afraid that in this depressed state I will make a bad choice. What should I do?" What would you say to her?

1. Get quiet. Get centered.
2. Know that love, acting in love, being in love, speaking with love paves the way to a love healing.
3. Be true to yourself and you cannot be false to anyone.
4. Be confident of your ability to make a wise decision.
5. Go ahead. Don't look back.

THE DECREEING METHOD

Have you tried the decreeing method? Caution: Be very careful about the words you use. Be concise. Write them down exactly as you plan to use them. Remember: Make your decree apply only for yourself, the highest good for you. To decree a thing is similar to speaking your word. It holds the power to clear long held-inner wounds. Find a time and place where you will not be disturbed for an hour. Center yourself in God's Light. Loudly speak your decree: **I shall decree a thing and it shall become a reality. I decree that I am free from all depression.** Then return to your meditative session. Pay attention to your changed view. If you are not completely clear, you may have to do it three times.

A decree works wonders to begin the action, but you have to do the minute-by-minute control over your thought or it will be like blowing in the wind. Once you have done your decree, do not allow yourself to think about the matter again. As much as we would like to believe that we are eternally placed in this pit of depression, this is not the Truth. By making a consciously determined effort, you can be free.

TRUST YOURSELF, TRUST GOD WITHIN

Life is not just a drama. Sometimes it's a trauma. I was walking down this path not realizing I was coming to a dead end. Every step I took was with great hope and faith that everything would turn out wonderfully in the end. It did not. The end came and I was there, puzzled, afraid, confused, following every lead, still a dead end. Many helping hands tried to save me, give me courage, direction and to point the way. To no avail. The dead end was still there, the walls surrounding me growing taller as I struggled. I turned back. In my emotional confusion I closed behind me the doors that had held a promise of escape. I was trapped: no way to turn, the walls too tall to climb, and my emotional state closed in, putting a lid over my head. No wisdom or creativity could penetrate. Why? Why is this happening to me? No answer came.

Question after question came to my mind. Why me? Why now? Why in this circumstance? What caused this action? Still no answer.

I am a great believer in cause and effect. For every effect there has to be an equal cause. Who was this happening to?

I questioned. It is happening to me. So who is the cause of my life. I am! For years I have blamed the events of my life on outside causes.

They did it unto me. Who this mythical "they" is, has changed from time to time. Again, "they" had done it unto me.

As I sat on my pity pot grieving over what might have been, and kicking poor little me for fooling myself that it ever could have been, a glimmer of light began to shine through the darkness. Trust, trust yourself. Trust God within you.

Be still, my aching heart. There is an answer. There is a way. Trust. When we come solely from the hurt, the ache, the anger, there is no answer or solution. Look within. The answer is there. God is working Its purpose out through us. And our purpose is not to be mired in negative conditions. Somewhere within you is the answer, is the way. We are not put here in life to" suffer the slings and arrows of outrageous fortune." We are here to overcome these appearances and reveal God's Truth in our lives. There is an answer!

Are you in confusion today? Do you know which way to turn? or to whom to turn?

Are you seeking answers as I did?

First, I learned that the answers are not "out there." They are in here. They are inside us in that secret place of the most high. God is revealing your path right now if you are listening, looking, seeking the answer. Clear away the debris of this situation. Clear out the anger, disappointment, fear, frustration, confusion, guilt, embarrassment, and depression. Let yourself be human. Let yourself make mistakes. They are of no consequence, if you learn from them and don't make them again. Forgive yourself. Forgive everyone who had a part in that painful scenario.

If you are asking why your prayers didn't work the answer is that they did work. Somehow your basic feelings and thoughts about this situation were its inevitable outcome.

It would be nice if life were like a drama on the stage, if you lived, laughed, loved or cried with the hero or heroine for an hour or two and then could return to your neat little world of light and love. Not so! Sometimes our lives are all too real. And our failures too graphic. Some times our direction becomes so clouded that we don't know which way to turn. This is a debilitating feeling. **There is an answer.**

Look inside you. Be still. Focus your attention to an inspiring word or saying, such as "Peace", "peace I leave with you. My peace I give unto you." (John 14:27) Allow the feeling of action in that statement to overcome any other thought. Pretend, if you have to, that peace can be like gold glitter sprinkling all over you and your situation, bringing peace to your mind and your life. As it falls sparkling down, all confusion dissipates, and you are at peace. Answers do not come through confusion; only through clear thinking can they come. So when your thought becomes clear, ask your questions. If you are still asking "Why did this have to happen to me?" you are wasting your clear thought. Ask instead, "Where do I go from here?"

Resist the temptation to react in some negative way at this time. It is normal for you to want to get even or seek revenge, but it is non-productive and will delay your healing and cloud your clear vision. Also, the Law of Cause and Effect will escalate the matter until it is unrecognizable. Better to take the blows and release the anger in an impersonal way (shouting to the wind or beating a pillow). Even crying to a friend shuts down their positive creative ideas for you and limits their effectiveness to council you. A call to your Licensed Practitioner will put your situation into proper perspective. Most Religious Science Churches have licensed Practitioners. You will help yourself and the situation immeasurably if you consult one.

You are not placed here on earth to suffer, be confused, disappointed or limited in any way. There is a place inside you that knows this is the Truth about you. You are a Divine Child of a loving ,beneficent God always within you, awaiting your call. Trust God within to guide you through this experience, and any other, safely. You are never alone.

The ever- present God lights your way and makes the crooked places straight. Look within you for the answer. Look inside you and expect a clear answer immediately. If it cannot penetrate your confusion at that time, ask your question again as you drop off to sleep.

I asked for a plan. I am used to operating by plan, one action after another toward my goals, so I asked the God within me as I dropped off to sleep. When I awoke in the morning, a plan was clearly in my mind and I wrote it down. More parts to this plan are coming as I clear my mind of confusion.

Getting through that confusion to peace of mind, and direction need to be your main goals at this time. Sometimes the confusion is so great the only thing that will divert your mind is a soap opera on television, a war movie or a romance novel. Watch it, read it, if it helps. Then when your mind is clear, put positive thoughts into your conscious mind such as: **this too shall pass** or **God is working its purpose out through me, now!** Continue to look for the good in the traumatic situation. Know that if one door shuts, a greater, more rewarding door is opening.

Take this time to do some of the things you have been putting off. Clean the cupboard, straighten up the garage, polish the car, visit your shut-in aunt. Get your mind into practical pursuits, and prepare yourself for bigger and better things ahead.

Nobody likes living in confusion, yet most of the people of the world live in confusion their entire lives, reeling from one trauma after another. If you have overcome much of life's confusion and frustration through study and practice of Spiritual Principles it can be quite a shock to experience them.

At this time we may be tempted to question our chosen path, and either condemn it (It doesn't work) or embrace it even more fully. My faith says that it does work and it is working now. Though I might not like my present experience of it, this is not all there is. There are greater blessings in store for me.

Resist the temptation to give up or throw in the towel on your dream. God is always working Its purpose out through you and me. This appearance may have been necessary to change your direction and open some new doors. Someone said to me, "You would never have given up the commitment you made to that situation. You had to be blasted out of it." And they were right. It took a great blast to loosen me from my "appointed" task and start me in another direction.

Living in confusion is not fun. It is life rending. Do the necessary things it takes to get past the confusion to peace of mind as quickly as you can. Healing takes place immediately once you're there.

Mental discipline is the answer. By consciously diverting our thoughts from the situation, we let some of the energy it has generated subside.

As metaphysicians we practice positive affirmations over and over to learn how to control our thought. Since our minds work similarly to the computer in this instance, the program we instill in our minds overrides all else. All the affirmation practice that we have done is most helpful when a challenge of great magnitude appears. Be gentle with yourself but firm. When you realize that you are again searching through the garbage, stop! Return to a simple affirmation. **I am God's perfect child. I am loved, successful and blessed. I remain at peace in all areas of my life.**

If the negative train of thought persists, it is helpful to wave your arms and proclaim, "I FORGIVE, I FORGIVE, I FORGIVE!" and then, "I RELEASE, I RELEASE, I RELEASE!" Immediately look at a peaceful scene or a picture of happy times. You will discover that a physical and mental release is the result. Review your positive affirmations again.

You may say that this is all well and good, but I know that my subconscious mind is not buying any of this as I'm still having nightmares re-enacting my trauma. Do not give up.

Little drops of water,
Little grains of sand
Make the mighty oceans
And the verdant land.

It may take some time, but persistence pays off. By reading materials of a positive nature before bedtime, you can even change your dreams.

Reward yourself by praising yourself when you have spent some time not thinking about the trauma. Say aloud, "I haven't thought about it all morning. Great! Wonderful!" Then get on with other more productive things. I recommend you start an all consuming project that captivates all your conscious thought. Become completely absorbed in it. Perhaps, learn how to work your computer in some new way. Take a class in computers to become more proficient. Practice that piece on the piano until it is memorized. Get that paintbox out and paint your masterpiece. Plant your garden. Put your body and mind to productive use. As your computer is limited in memory, so is you mind.

Do something that restores your faith in yourself. Give yourself something to think about and talk about instead of the trauma. Get out among congenial friends who are not likely to bring up old situations. Being reclusive at this time may impede your healing. Get out and be with people of like mind. Practice being in the present moment with them.

Let yourself enjoy the moments of clarity. The more opportunities you make to be clear of thought, the more you will release the confusion.

Where are you seeking to find help? Have you gone to friends and family? Have you sought assistance from AA or professional counselors? May I suggest that the more answers you get, the more confused you get. Even if you take a consensus of opinions and choose the best or most promising, there can be repercussions later. Often family and friends will be unhappy if you don't take their advice. Free advice isn't free; it usually has strings attached.

The real solution to any question is never found out there. The answer is within you. The Source is always within. As you experience more time of clear thought, the help you need will be revealed to you. Many a person has had the help they need in hand and did not realize it because of confused thinking. You and the inner you know more about the situation than you could tell anyone. Your inner eye, when clear, will see things quite differently. That which you know and need to know is within. Ask your inner self for it. Here are some steps to remove confusion and return to clarity of mind.

FAKE IT UNTIL YOU MAKE IT

Use these steps to bring balance (centerness) back to your thought and world even before they seem to be possible.

Fake it until you make it.

1. Refrain from why is this happening to me? thinking.
2. No matter how impossible the solution to your trauma may seem to be, THERE IS AN ANSWER, THERE IS A WAY.
3. It is no one's fault. Accept the responsibility for your life and move on.
4. Resist the temptation to get even.
5. Stop blaming anyone, especially yourself.
6. Acknowledge that you are human and make mistakes.
7. Let moving from confusion to clarity be your goal.
8. Keep the faith. It does work. Prayer does work.
9. Set a plan into action to keep physically and mentally active. When you are into the garbage, do some physical or mental activity to divert your attention.
10. Praise yourself when you have succeeded in staying out of your trauma for a time.
11. Practice being in the moment.
12. Seek the answer within you. Trust yourself. Trust God.
13. Try prayer. Meditation helps.
14. Read something of a spiritual nature that lifts you up out of the problem on a daily basis. Read to saturation.
15. Center yourself on a regular basis.
16. TRUST GOD.

Use these sixteen steps as your plan to remove all vestages of depression. Say again with me, **DEPRESSION BE GONE!**

Notes

Chapter 4

RETURN TO THE SOURCE

SO THE OLD STUFF CAME UP AGAIN. What triggered it? Either unfinished business, memories, seeing someone who reminded you or something inside of you. When this occurs, you know that it isn't over yet. All the hopelessness, anger, fear, depression and self condemnation have returned like it was yesterday. Resist the temptation to react. Stop acting on that old condition. It takes time to cleanse the inner Temple that has been defaced. Be gentle with yourself. Let off some of that angry energy. Let yourself shout, scream, cry (in private). When the energy is spent, center yourself in Spirit. Return to your God self. Return to the Source. Read the 16 steps in Chapter 3 to get out of depression over again and do them as if you have never done them before. (You may have to do this exercise several times.) Affirm: **My vision is clear. My purpose is revealed to me.** Focus your attention away from confusion to clarity.

The danger of sharing your pain with someone near and dear to you is that they take on some of the burden. Later, when you are over the matter to a great degree, trying to help you, your dear one can bring it back by their reaction or sharing their view of the situation. Lifetime prejudices or mind sets can become difficult obstacles for our loved ones, and they may never forgive the person or situation that hurt you. We are like mirrors to our dear ones. When we are upset and share it with them they reflect it right back to us. The problem can be escalated again and again, as they work their way through it. Their view of it can limit you later on when you least expect it. "You remember what the result was the last time you did this?" your loved one might say.

The best advice I can give is to call your Licensed Religious Science Practitioner and get a Spiritual Mind Treatment. Treatment has a way of clearing the mind and revealing your next step without the negative boomerang effect.

WHEN THE DARK NIGHT APPEARS

An unexpected call came that opened a glimmer of a way to go. "Hallelujah!" A moment before all was dark, like the dark night of the soul is described to be. Now, a new day is dawning, a light at the end of the black tunnel. "Peace, patience, take each step as it comes," you tell yourself.

You begin telling yourself that you are worthy of the greatest good, that God is indeed working Its purpose out through you, in you, as you, is you.

The physical world as yet does not reflect this new picture. There is much to be done to close the action. So you reluctantly begin. The paper work sends you swirling back into that dark black pit as you try to document the action that has gone before.

Echoes of old memories of the good times and the shame, the joys and the sorrows, the blessings and the disappointments put you back into that black tunnel again. You struggle to find your way in this hopelessness. God is still within you awaiting your call. So you scream, "God, help me!" And the help comes.

You are finished with that reminder of old times. Review it quickly for details and send it off with as much of a blessing as you can muster.

As your depression and confusion return, you again start through the 16 steps. Reading something of an uplifting nature to begin seems to help the most. Let new ideas permeate your being. Get a new slogan. **I am the master of my ship, I am the master of my destiny. I get back on that horse and ride it this time. I am strong. I have the faith to overcome. I prepare myself for my next spiritual assignment.** By reprogramming your mind, you are able to complete the tasks at hand.

This time the paper review of the past experience was uplifting. Being objective about a situation has that effect. The work was done quickly and easily. What accomplish-ments! I was not a failure! I was a complete success! (you realize as you really look at what you have accomplished). What a good feeling inside! A definite healing is taking place.

A man came to me in great depression of the soul. He had tried numerous methods to lift this black cloud, to no avail. It seemed he had lost his faith in the goodness and loving kindness of God. Though he was an advanced student of metaphysics, it no longer held anything for him. Somehow he had given his Power away. This is quite common when one attaches himself to a guru. He had worshipped his teacher far beyond that which a student needs to do, and he married her. When their marriage began to break up as their interests grew apart, he was unwilling to see the situation, holding on for dear life. He compromised himself over and over in order to continue the marriage. His inner belief system was challenged. All that he had learned or proved was discarded. When he finally came for assistance, it was many years later in the next marriage. The cloud still had not cleared. His new wife realized his need and encouraged his search for the answer.

The answer became clear on one sparkling day. The Guru is within you. You are the greatest, wisest, teacher you will ever find. Within you are all the answers and the power to bring them into your conscious mind.

My recommendation to this man: Restudy all the materials that you studied as a student with your ex-wife. If you begin to hear her voice saying the words, read those passages aloud so that your inner ear hears them in your voice. Put them into your memory as your own voice. Reclaim your power!

Hear yourself affirm your own positive affirmations. Rebuild your faith in yourself and in God.

The Light came on immediately within this man and he left with his Power restored.

We all tend to worship our spiritual teachers. Particularly when we are just beginning on our path. If you have become disenchanted with your teacher, minister or guru, remember: YOU ARE THE GREATEST, WISEST, TEACHER YOU WILL EVER FIND. Within you are all the answers you will ever need to master your life purpose.

THE GURU IS YOU. Injuries from overreliance on teachers or gurus are most debilitating. Some people take several life times to recover their faith.

If this is your situation, you can change it today.

REMEMBER: THE GURU IS YOU.

Notes

Chapter 5

THE BALANCE

When traumatic occurrences happen in our lives we tend to get into the self-evaluation mode. We try to evaluate our actions that led up to the problem. It is easy to blame others or depreciate ourselves. We walk a tightrope walk with dangers on either side. Stepping too far into self-depreciation brings about depression and the endless night of darkness. On the other hand, blaming others all the time limits our development our ability to learn from our mistakes. Self-evaluation allows for a review of the road just traveled in an objective view towards understanding, correction and healing. All must be kept in perfect balance.

One of the first things that is thrown out of balance at times of trauma is our physical schedule: eating, sleeping and exercising. Consciously return to your normal habits. If they were not exemplary, change them until you are truly nurturing your body. The outer world of experiences does affect our bodily functions, so making an effort to bring balance to the body will pay off as strength, energy, vitality and will affect your overall view of your life.

True balance can only be experienced when we look at ourselves and our lives from a higher perspective. We enjoy flying in an airplane as it gives the impression that we are leaving all our problems behind. While climbing up in altitude, objects such as cars and houses seem smaller, and our problems fall away. This feeling can be consciously invoked when you meditate. Daily meditation puts our everyday lives into order; puts the happenings into a perspective: This is not necessarily the truth or this too shall pass. Practice daily meditation, and you will soon discover your life experiences will fall into a more positive, more successful, and more dependable pattern.

PIGEON HOLE THINKING

Set aside a block of time (especially when the crisis is new) such as ten minutes each hour that you will devote to thinking about the matter. I call this pigeon hole thinking. You put off thinking about the matter until a set time and do not allow your mind to dwell on it until then. As time goes, on you may decide to think about the trauma for a short time in the morning after your meditation time, and at night before you meditate, leaving your mind clear the rest of the time to go about daily business. This frees you. Your mind allows you a space for normalcy. Try to do whatever business is needed when your mind is the most calm and free of turmoil .

Know that you are always led to make the right and perfect choice. Greater wisdom than you have ever known is acting on your behalf through you, when you attend to business in a peaceful mode. If we are here on this pathway in this lifetime to live, learn, love, laugh, listen and be happy, and free from depression, LEARNING is a major purpose. If learning is what we are here to do, then mistakes are just a part of that. When we go through a trial in life and make a mistake, it is important to take an objective view towards the lesson to be learned or correction to be made.

There is a larger picture which we do not always see until we are past the problem. Sometimes we can look back and see the road we have just traveled to get to where we are now. Then it all makes sense.

If it is a question of worthiness that appears, let me assure you that you are always worthy of God's love and blessings. All the good of Heaven awaits your acceptance of it.

Are you still putting yourself down? "How could I have been so stupid to be duped." "Why didn't I see the outcome?"

Keep a balance. Immediately put into your mind thoughts reassuring yourself of your intent at the beginning of this business. It was good. It was intended as a blessing for all concerned, including yourself

Remember: God is working Its purpose out through you. Say: **Only Good goes from me and only Good returns to me. The greatest gift I can give is to be a conductor of God's love and peace.**

I AM BALANCED.

Chapter 6

WHAT DO I DO NOW?

IS THIS ALL THERE IS FOR ME? Every moment of every day is a new beginning. Assess where you are right now in each area of your life: health, career, relationship, level of consciousness, happiness, and success toward your goal. Am I still susceptible to times of depression? Are mood swings still happening on a regular basis?

Perceive this to be your base line, your beginning. Pick one area of your life that you are dissatisfied with to give your attention to first. Get yourself centered. Ask yourself, What is my greatest dream or desire in this area? Write it out in full. Somewhere deep inside yourself you know the answer. Bring it to your conscious mind. If you choose to make that your goal, ask yourself, What do I do first? Then go about your life looking for the means to take that first step. It will be revealed to you. You may notice that you have to take a giant step; as in mounting your horse, you have to step up into the stirrup. As much as we'd like it to be given to us on a platter, often we have to make the commitment. The first move is stepping up.

This may be the time to stand on your own two feet. We all need to do this from time to time. Know that you are capable, dependable and able to make it yourself. You can step forth confidently in this knowledge. Trust yourself. Trust your wisdom.

REMEMBER: all answers, all direction come from within. You validate them by your actions. This takes faith. Faith in yourself and faith in God. What about getting back on the horse that bucked you off? Is that feasible? Take some time and look at the completed plan. The picture may still be in your consciousness. Look at the end result. Ask yourself if just changing the horse you were riding would bring you to the same conclusion. Or is there another way to reach your goal? A little exploring on your inner picture of your life plan at this time may be quite beneficial. Try to keep your mind open and explore various means to reach your end result. THERE IS A WAY! And it will be revealed to your conscious mind, if you can just stay open and out of confusion. At this time using the mantras THERE IS A WAY AND IT IS BEING REVEALED TO ME, NOW! contains great power.

Continue to seek the answer on the inner, and allow it to be revealed as unexpected opportunity to the outer conscious mind. Be willing to recognize it and be ready to act on it when it is presented.

I will not say that if you don't recognize it the first time it is presented that it will not come again. It may come again and again, until you accept it and act on it.

GET BUSY

NOW, get busy! Get on with your life. If you have to overbook yourself, get busy. Get busy out in the world doing for others. Fill your time with good works. There is nothing better to clear the mind of its depression than to get involved in some worthy cause. At first choose something that is totally unrelated to your trauma, to which you can give your complete attention. Saturate yourself in this project.

Find a way to help someone, even if you feel you have no skills or are lacking in money or strength. You can visit someone in the hospital, chauffeur someone to the grocery store or the doctor's office. Volunteer your time with Hospice or the local library. Elementary schools often need volunteer aid's in the classroom to teach children to read. Look around. There is something you can do for others.

Perhaps nothing appeals to you. You have more questions than you do answers that loom greater and greater over your head, becoming an uncontrollable monster. It is easier to remain in the problem than it is to overcome it and move on. Staying in the problem, planning retribution or retaliation does keep your mind occupied, but has great repercussions in future times that you may not wish to experience. Really there is no justification for passing your hurt on to someone else. Stop it at your door. Do not pass it on.

While you are busy physically and mentally, continue to ask your questions.

Who am I?
Why am I here?
Where do I go from here?
What do I do next?
What is the greatest solution to this problem?

REMEMBER: There is a power for good in the Universe and you are using it right now. Use this power on all levels. Use this power to get yourself busy. An active mind is a healthy and clear mind.

Use this power to keep yourself centered in Spirit. Confusion has no place when your focus is on God. The hidden place within you wherein God resides is always untouched by the world. Great peace and renewed spiritual awareness is the result of being in tune with your inner spirit.

Use this power to answer your greatest questions. When your greatest questions are answered, often your next step is clearly revealed. Learn to listen and then record the messages that come to you in your Book of Life. Keeping a written record of important messages or directions is very important. Start a Book of Life and put these inspirational ideas there for future reference

Use this power for good to reveal your purpose and the next step toward your goal. Listen and let the pictures come. Visualize and record the plan as it is revealed. The reason for your former experience may be shown as your flashes of wisdom stream forth.

Nothing that has occurred is outside of God. In some wonderful way a greater good is the result, when you resist the temptation to add negative actions and energy to the situation.

When the Master Jesus was arrested in Gethsemane, Peter drew his sword and cut off a soldier's ear in his defense. Jesus could not allow a retaliatory action to occur. He immediately healed the soldier. What you do and think at the time of trauma determines how quickly you recover and how clearly your next step is revealed. It can not come when your thought is in confusion, hurting, angry, fearful, or frustrated.

Consciously choose to keep your body and mind active, alert and aware in a different kind of activity. Putting yourself on hold until the negative action subsides and you are back in your center. Resist the temptation to go into hibernation so that when the next step is revealed, you will be ready.

Your Eternal Plan has not changed, nor is it sidetracked. This next step has awaited your turning to it for some time.

There is always a way to continue. It matters not what has happened before. Where you are in consciousness now is the vital question. Every conscious thought has power, and the Universe acts on our conscious and unconscious thought. Though it may seem difficult to monitor (control) your thoughts, it must be done. To benefit to the greatest degree from your experience, a self-disciplined thought pattern is a wonderful benefit at this time.

Our actions stem from our thoughts. When we have a well-disciplined mind we can depend upon, we will not be incurring further reason to be hurt. Practice some of the old lessons in self-discipline. See no evil, hear no evil, speak no evil about anybody, any place or any thing. This may not be easy, but it is important. Hurtful, harmful words and retaliatory thought-pictures are just as dangerous as cutting off an ear.

Choose your thoughts carefully. Control you actions, and know that what you give out you will get back, even in times of trauma.

So get busy in a different area of your life that draws your complete attention to it, and be patient. The muddy water will clear. Soon all will be revealed to you.

PREPARE YOURSELF

Meanwhile, prepare yourself. Take a class. Get active. Keep yourself visible so that you can see, the Universe can see, and those about you can see, that you are in control of your life and proceeding along your way with confidence. There is no better way to heal yourself in body, mind and spirit than to prepare yourself for your next opportunity.

Play the game WHAT IF? What if?

I were offered an opportunity to

____

____

____

Affirm: I'M PREPARED. I AM READY!
Why not? Do not worry how it is to come about. Just know that it is now a reality.

Spend some time getting your clothes ready. Get your car ready, get your house in order so that spending more time away would not be difficult. Get your physical life in order.

Put your time to good use. Try to project into the future what would be helpful when your opportunity comes.

Do it. Prepare yourself for your great opportunity.
Knowing what you know about this business, prepare yourself.

A widower desired a wife. not just any wife, but one he could give himself to completely, one that would be loving, and kind and have mutual interests.

His list of her qualities was quite long.

One day as he was going over his list the thought came to him, "I believe that one draws to ones self that which one is." So he looked at the list of attributes he desired in a wife and discovered that he himself did not qualify to have such a wife. Immediately, he set about changing his habits of mind and living style to match the kind of wife he desired. Two main attributes kept echoing in his mind: loving and giving. Now, this man had never given anything in his life, so he started helping others when the opportunity presented itself.

His desire for a positive, pleasant, gracious lady brought him to his local church. About that time, the church was having a fundraising. He volunteered his time and talent as a fixit man to be auctioned off to the highest bidder. To his surprise, there was quite a competition. It seemed that everyone needed help.

The winner turned out to be his winner for life, as the lady who won his services, won his heart.

He had to change a great deal before he was ready.

PREPARE YOURSELF!

Chapter 7

CHOICES

You may think that you are boxed in on all sides. That all is lost. That you have no way to turn. It is easy to stay in this limited place. In fact it is easier to stay there where you are than it is to remove yourself from it. Some people never lift their eyes to greater possibilities in their lifetime.

Are you ready? Are you ready to change your life experience? If you are, you must choose, consciously choose a better way. I assure you that there is a better way, a better life, a happier state, a greater expression, and it is available at your choosing. You do not have to know what it is at this moment, but the very fact that you are choosing, consciously choosing, a better life, assures you that it will be revealed.

Great fear was expressed a number of years ago that Big Brother (governmental thought control) would be a future method of controlling populations. Several countries experimented with this method by brainwashing, mental repression, independent expression and censoring news media. It did not work. Many of those Nazi, Communistic countries are in dysfunction now. They did not take into consideration a person's inalienable right to freedom of thought and choice.

People became suspicious of all news media put out by their government; held their peace around those who might betray them, and sought the truth with tenacity. No kind of thought control has proved successful except that instigated by the person him or herself.

YOU HAVE THE POWER TO CONTROL YOUR WORLD THROUGH YOUR THOUGHT. Your thought contains great power. The way you look at your life, the beliefs you hold about it, everything that happens to you, happens through you. So great is your thought that you have the power to change your life by the very thoughts you hold. It rests in your power to choose. Today, you can choose your thoughts about your experience. How wonderful that is. You can choose the way you look at depression and consciously change it.

LOOK FOR THE BLESSING

Take a look at the trauma or drama that just torpedoed you. What if there is a blessing hiding there somewhere?

I know this may seem impossible, but stretch you mind a bit. If there could possibly be a blessing there for you to see, choose to look. Choose to look at the action with new eyes. Ask yourself if there might be something good coming out of this that you haven't seen as yet.

When you can see the happening as a blessing in disguise, you are on the healing way. Choose to look for the good. Praise it when it is clear to you. Your gift of choice is a precious gift. Guard it with all your might. The ability to choose your own thought contains great power within it.

Thank God! No one can take that away from you.

We have many choices to make every day. We have been making choices since birth and perhaps before birth. They range from the simplest, what I shall think about this moment, to choosing to breathe, thus continuing life. The power of choice is precious and should not be taken lightly.

Many people are afraid to make choices. Are you one of them? Are you afraid to make a choice because it might be a mistake? It is true that the mental and emotional status of the person making a choice does affect the outcome. This may seem a great responsibility to some. Let's start with something simple: the choice to think positive, good thoughts. You may say that that is not as simple as it sounds. This may seem so difficult since you have been caught up in depressed thinking for such a long time.

The secret to healing the dark cloud that lingers, hanging heavily over your head, to turn away from the difficulty. Consciously choose to turn away. Happiness is a choice that we make every day. The longer we choose to dwell on the problem, the longer that problem will hold us in its grasp.

This self-feeding monster tends to grow the more we give it power. We give it power when we allow ourselves to think about it.

A helpful approach that I use instead of worrying and contributing to the power of the issue is to realize no matter what I may be facing, it won't continue forever. The old saying comes to mind: this too shall pass. When I repeat this in the face of the problem, I immediately feel better. The anxiety begins to lift.

Are you existing on a DEFERRED LIVING PLAN? Many of us appear to be doing just that. I'll be happy when I find my right mate, or my new house is finished. I'm overdue for a raise. I'll be happy when it comes through.

Happiness is a NOW situation. Happiness happens right now, in the situation that you are in and, most importantly, it is a choice you are making every moment of every day. I believe that happiness is a conscious choice we make moment by moment, day by day.

Why do we prune our fruit trees? To get rid of the old growth, remove unproductive branches that will not be able to bear the weight of the new crop, to take out the dead wood. These are just a few of the reasons we prune our fruit trees. Pruning is good for our trees. Do you suppose it might be good for us also?

The subjective or subconscious mind acts on our thoughts and our statements about ourselves. "I wanna be, I may be, I hope to be, I wish to be, I try to be" are all tomorrow's wishes not today's affirmations. Positive statements like: '**I am happy. I am healthy. I am prosperous. I am surrounded by loving people. I am loving.** Thoughts held in the conscious mind will eventually imprint on the subjective or subconscious mind and begin to create on the outer what is imprinted on the inner.

A Practitioner friend of mine shared with me her experience in looking for a job. She was out of work for a long time and desperately needed work. She had looked and looked. She was tired of filling out applications. She had tried hard to stay positive in the situation of interview after interview. She maintained that the right and perfect place, a place she could be happy in, was looking for her and her special talents.

One day as she was driving home from another interview she said to herself, "OK God, I give up. I'm too tired. I can't do this myself. YOU help me find the right job." And she opened her heart to the Infinite.

At that moment an envelope dropped in her lap from the sun visor where she had put it a few days before. She opened it. Inside was a letter from an employment agency notifying her that a job was listed to work with animals in the city Humane Society Shelter. As soon as she read it, she knew it was exactly what she was to do. She loves animals and has a special rapport with them. They trust her immediately. The answer was clear.

She applied and got her dream job. She has worked at this job for a number of years. She loves her work. She affirms, "I am happy. I love my work."

Our minds work this way: Beliefs or ideas held for a period of time create patterns in our mind. Regularly affirming that which you desire to experience will eventually become etched in the mind patterns and will become a reality in your body, mind and affairs. This is how we create our world and our experiences. To change the patterns that have been previously set takes many repetitions of positive ideas before the old pattern is replaced. Many repetitions of the positive affirmation is needed until a habit of positive thought is created.

How can you tell what your present mind-set pattern is? Here's the test. Look out at your world. Look at the degree of depression you are experiencing. All these are indications of your mind-set pattern. Change seems to come slowly. But regular, conscious effort will make a difference.

AFFIRM: HEALTH: I am healthy. My body functions excellently. It is strong, dependable and filled with energy.

ABUNDANCE: I am abundant. Every need is met before it's time. All my bills are paid. I am confident of my continued prosperity. Money is good. I have plenty to spend and to share.

RELATIONSHIPS: I am happy with myself and all my relationships are loveships. I give love to everyone unconditionally. I receive love back in many wonderful ways. I am loved. I am happy!

SUCCESS: I am success. Success in all areas of my life is my reality, now! Everything I do is successful. I acknowledge my successful life.

EMOTIONAL LEVEL: Emotionally, I am calm, peaceful and confident of myself. I reveal the God within to myself and to others. Nothing can rock my boat. I return to that secret place within on a regular basis and live in that great peace. I am blessed eternally.

SPIRITUAL LEVEL: I am always seeking the highest level of consciousness. As I overcome the lesser, the greater is revealed to me, today. Every day I acknowledge that it is not I who doeth the works, but the Father within me. THANK YOU GOD!

You can write your own affirmations. They will have greater power if you put them in your own words.

WHAT DO YOU CHOOSE? Know that your choice is far reaching. Your choice makes your life what it is today and in the future. Your choice wields great power.

CHOOSE TO MAKE THE NECESSARY CHANGES IN YOUR THOUGHT, TODAY!

Chapter 8

GOD'S WILL

Interpreting God's will has been the basis of many world religions. Defining God's will has been important for many people throughout history. And God's will has been so misinterpreted.

WHAT IS GOD'S WILL FOR YOU AND ME? God's will for every man, woman and child is: to live, laugh, love, learn, listen, be healthy and happy. How else could it be?

First, God's will is for us to live, to express life to the greatest degree. What does that mean to you? To me that means a strong healthy body that is capable of doing all that I ask of it, a life with a purpose that is rewarding and centered. It means a pathway that is clear and reachable that sustains myself and all those whom I influence along the way.

To live does not mean eat, drink and be merry for tomorrow you shall die. It does mean to live as your highest self, being your greatest self as often as possible. To make choices and actions from the GREAT ME rather than the

LITTLE ME to act instead of reacting.

Also, to consider this vehicle that has been provided for your use as sacred. Honor your physical temple by not just saying all things in moderation, as has been taught, but "I put no thing into my body temple that will defile or injure it so that it will serve me well and give me many years of trouble free service" You would not put water into your gasoline tank, so choose only the best most healthful foods and drinks. Preservation of the body temple is part of self-love and self-discipline. Live, act and be God's expression of Light to this world. Live that way.

The Creator God created this body and the bodies of all other humans after a plan. It is clear that there was an original or beginning design that was followed for all with a few variations to make it interesting. Duplicate copies would have been a complete bore and we would have sought to become individual immediately. Yet we are enough alike to make generalizations as to body structure. And we live. We are alive.

We live in a world that is orderly, dependable and governed by Spiritual, Mental and Natural-Physical Laws.

We have great power over our life. We can use this power to enhance and bless ourselves and our lives, or we can do away with our life completely and every variation in between. We can vacillate between using this power constructively or destructively.

We are not robots, but have the power of free thought. Using free thought, we can build a happy, joyous life of our choice, or the opposite. Not everyone knows this Truth; lives of great limitation are the result.

LAUGH

God's will for us is to laugh. The power of laughter is so great that it will heal all manner of disease, and we can use it or not. Certainly, laughter invoked in a tense situation will bring about a change in attitude. We've all used this to improve a situation, to change negative energy into positive. Put the healing power of laughter into your daily plan and discover how beneficial it can be for you and your situation. Keep a joke book around that you enjoy. Put comedy into your TV watching schedule. Look for the lighter side of your trauma. I'm sure it's there to be found. Find something to laugh about every day, and you will be delighted to find that you are healing your body, mind and spirit at a phenomenal rate of speed, putting your trauma into perspective.

LOVE

God's will for us is to love and be loved. The Master Jesus said, "Love your enemy as yourself. Do good to those who hate you or persecute you."

The first person whom you must learn to love is YOURSELF. The power of love is useless if you don't love yourself. Truly you are a lovable person and God loves you irrevocably and unconditionally. No matter what you may have thought about yourself, or been taught about yourself you are worthy of all the love of God and of people, all people. You deserve all the love that is given to you. Accept it as your birthright. You are worthy of it!

LEARN

Learning, learning, so much to learn. Is that how you feel?

Actually, you have already learned a lot: how to work this body, how to get along in the sandbox called life, learning the academic skills to become a decision making responsible human being. We all have accomplished at least this much.

Many times we have been presented with the task of taking the responsibility for our actions and choices and we have learned perhaps over and over the importance of this.

Self-control and self-discipline are lessons presented with regularity. Keeping our thoughts, words and deeds on the highest level and our vision of life as heaven on earth takes control and discipline.

God's will for us is to learn. If this life experience here on earth is like a schoolroom and lessons of our choice are provided for us to grow in consciousness and discover God to a greater degree, then we will learn. Have you noticed that certain experiences seem to repeat themselves in your life? You will discover that they will continue to repeat until you overcome the cause. So learn what is there for you to learn, and move onward. To the degree that you have learned the lesson or overcome the problem, it will return usually in a lesser form, but return it does. If you have learned the lesson completely, it will never be presented to you again in this life time or the next.

Learn to use the Principles in every area of your life. The Principles or Universal law works automatically on your mind pattern and beliefs. We hold in our mind certain ideas. Universal Law says YES and acts as if they are the truth. It does not say whoa, back up. That's not good for you. It merely says yes and acts upon those beliefs. That is why an examination of our thoughts and beliefs is so important.

Are you feeling blocked, limited or in confusion? Are you worried about competition, scarcity, lack or falling back into depression? Begin a conscious plan to remove these fears from your consciousness. Affirm: **I am unlimited. There is ample good for all. There is no competition, scarcity or lack in God's Universe. I am free from all depression forever.**

We come by spiritual understanding from many different and varied paths; a very clear dream, psychic experience, read a book, or hear it on TV, or find it in AA. Some of us come from the traditional church, seeking the Truth. Or you may have know it from childhood, that the world is not quite what it seems to be. Each of us came step by step to our present state of consciousness. Now, it is time for the next step.

Learn to turn from the external world to the God Within seeking the Light that is always glowing brightly within you. No matter what our teachers, books, or guru's have said, we have had to discover our inner Light for ourselves. As you have learned this you may have found that you are experiencing a new and greater, more divine life than ever before. It becomes an all consuming desire to use your power to accomplish a permanent stability in all areas of your life and new steps in consciousness can do it!

REMEMBER: **God does not have to give us Light. God has already given it. And God is it.**

Lessons in spiritual understanding are to discover who and what you are. You are a Powerful Spiritual Being. All the power of the Universe is at your command.

Learning what the Law of the Universe is and how to use it is an important purpose in this life for many people. The

Law of Cause and Effect works automatically on your thoughts, words and deeds.

There is no way to stop it except at its source: **your thought.** Your thought is the cause of all that happens in your body, relationships, business affairs and world. How important it is to learn to control your thought every minute of every day! In doing so you can dismiss that depression with a determined, "Be Gone!" and plant in your thought ideas of joy, happiness and peace. You can do it! I know you can! This idea contains great promise to anyone who has mastered the sickness of drug or alcohol addiction. You may not have to suffer with it to such a debilitating degree in the next life-time. Certainly, planting ideas of **"I can lick this thing that has depressed me"** will set out a pattern of confidence in yourself, in your ability to overcome future challenges.

So when challenges come to your life, put them into a perspective that This too shall pass and I can overcome even this. Learn to choose the highest and best no matter what it is.

The Power to choose is yours; and using it to discipline or direct your thoughts is an important lesson we are all here to learn. Begin today on a program of challenging your thoughts and only let the "good" thoughts that you want to experience in your life become etched in your memory.

REMEMBER: **The Universe (God) is for you.**

LISTEN

God's will for us is to listen. How can we recognize our pathway if we don't listen to that still small voice within us? LISTEN! Spend time in the silence communing with the God within you. Learn to listen to that still small voice whispering from within telling you who you are, why you are here and how to express more peace, love and joy in your world. It is from the great within, the part of you that is in touch with the wisdom of the ages. The voice of God to the world. Listen, there are great things for you to do here in this lifetime. Listen and act on that wisdom knowing that God's purpose is being served. Meditation is true listening.

Daily meditation contains so many blessings for your inner self and your outer world. If you have never tried to meditate or only do so occasionally, put it into your regular schedule. Actually, we need to learn to live on the inner, higher level most of the time. When we can do this, our outer world becomes blissful. All the wisdom and good judgment you will ever need is available to you, awaiting your asking in your inner connection to Universal Mind. All you have to do is ask, believing that you have the answer, and it is given.

No matter what situation you find yourself in, the greatest wisdom of the Universe is yours immediately. If you have practiced meditation as an automatic method of centering yourself, you have developed a great power over your mind, body and life experiences.

A student of mine was in a terrible automobile accident. The day started out quite innocently. She and her granddaughter discovered they were out of milk so on this foggy morning they set out to the store to get some. Their home was in a remote area, five miles from the nearest neighbor. It was a winding dirt road, and she lost her bearings and zigged instead of zagged. Her bright red truck rolled over the embankment, and over again. Her door opened and then closed on her forearm.

Her four-year-old granddaughter was unhurt as she had been strapped in her seat. She knew her own face was bleeding and her chest hurt. The child found the bottle of water and wiped her grandmother's face. She knew that no one would be passing on the road until much later in the day. From time to time she heard the sound of a chain saw in the distance. She was able to reach the horn with her toe and honked it. As soon as she was able to gather her wits about her, she centered them in white light. It wasn't long before their dog, Mitzie, found them. She ordered her to go get help at the neighbors. Mitzie did not want to leave them, but finally did as she was bid.

The neighbor related that from time to time during that day he had heard a strange horn honking and finally came to investigate. On meeting Mitzie on the path, he was lead directly to the upside down red truck.

The jaws of life were summoned to open the top of the truck and the grand daughter was taken home by neighbors.

During the women's long wait , she remembers only one thing. Someone said to her, "Come to Center," Which was the familiar key she had used for years in her mediation. She felt no more discomfort, her mind was clear and she remained conscious.

Final outcome: though the doctors recommended many things including amputation of her forearm at the wrist as it was about a quarter inch thick where the door had closed on it, she refused. Due to meditation and Spiritual Mind Treatment, her arm was back in use in a little over a year's time. All visible signs of the accident were gone.

All time spent in meditation has value. Turning to that Higher Power within heals bodies, minds, life's experiences and sets you on a new path of joy, peace of mind and great inner happiness.

BE HEALTHY

BE HEALTHY! You might say, I would if I could. It's God's will that we be healthy, else our bodies would not be programmed to heal themselves and wellness just a faint hope. A healed perfect body would not be possible if it were not God's will for everyone of us. The body has the ability to heal itself. Modern medicine merely assists in that effort. Radiant health at any age is the expectation and possibility we all have. Rejoice in this Truth. God's will for us is to live free of physical limitation of any kind.

Lastly, BE HAPPY! as God intended his divine children to be. How else is there to be? Life is a precious gift and we are supposed to be happy in it.

BE HAPPY

God's will for us is to be happy. I'll bet you never looked at it this way. GOD WANTS US TO BE HAPPY! else why would we be here? And happiness in not unattainable. It is simply a mental attitude. You can choose to be happy at any time, in any situation or life experience. Your attitude is the key. So BE HAPPY! Choose to be happy! God's greatest will for you is to be happy. How else would a loving parent feel? I'm sure your greatest desire for your children is that they be happy in this life. God's desire for his children is to be happy. How wonderful this is!

So, if you are not happy, why not? If your answer is immediately that someone or something or some experience outside of you is the reason for your unhappiness, you are looking in the wrong place. Happiness is an inside job. You have to be happy on the inside before you will find happiness out in the world. Start where you are and begin to look for reasons to be happy. Choose to be happy in the circumstance you find yourself right now; no matter what is going on in your life or your inner world. Choose to think happy thoughts and look for reasons to be happy with yourself and everyone and everything in your world.

Ask yourself, "What would it take for me to be happy right now, here in this place and time?" I don't mean for you to look out at your world and ask that question. Ask the inner self. The greatest answer you will ever get is within you. Look inside. That is all it takes. Look at the evidence within you. You are so unique, so special, so wonderful in every way. You deserve to be happy.

Start by framing pictures in your mind of reasons to think happy thoughts. Look at yourself with happy eyes. See yourself as God sees you, his blessed child.

God's will could never be that you be judged, unhappy, belittled, diminished, depressed or any less than who you really are, and you are A DIVINE CHILD OF GOD!

What is God's will for you? To live, laugh, love, learn, listen, be healthy and be happy. Today say to yourself: **DEPRESSION, BE GONE! I choose to believe that God's will for me is GOOD: the highest, happiest, and best of all possible lives. That is my life right now!**

Chapter 9

HAPPINESS IS A CHOICE

Abraham Lincoln is purported to have said, "Most people are about as happy as they make up their minds to be."

HOW HAPPY ARE YOU?

1. Are you happy and satisfied with your health, weight, strength, your body?

2. Are you happy with your work, activities, hobbies?

3. Are you happy about your supply, money, and living situation?

4. Are you happy with your close relationships? Do you feel loved, appreciated, secure and blessed?

5. Are you at peace with yourself. Are you happy with yourself?

6. Are you happy with the level of consciousness you have attained?

7. Are you happy?

Mark Twain once remarked, "Drag your thoughts away from your troubles........by the ears, by the heels, or any other way you can manage it. It's the healthiest thing a body can do."

This may seem so difficult. But until we learn to discipline our thoughts out of the problem and turn to the opposite, the good, we will be feeding that endless circle of unhappiness.

Every unhappy thought tends to cultivate another unhappy thought until you have an endless train. Stop it immediately and place the good your desire into your thought.

HAPPINESS IS A CHOICE

How happy are you in these areas of your life? On a scale of 1-10 rate yourself. One being very little to not happy at all, ten being very happy.

Physical Health __________

Mental Health __________

Prosperity ______________

Success _________________

Relationships ____________

Emotional Level __________

Spiritual Level ___________

Look at all the less than 10 scores. Remember what caused you to mark it that way.

Write an affirmation (short positive statement) for each area that you rated lower than you desire it to be.

Post the affirmation in a prominent place and review it often. Keep a log of good thoughts and happenings. As the situation begins to improve, record the GOOD only the GOOD!

Do you feel you have to pursue happiness? Our Constitution says that it is our right. The pursuit of happiness often gives us the feeling that we are chasing the impossible dream of some future time or place: I'll be happy when I move into another house. I'll be happy when I get a better job. I'll be happy when I find my right mate. I'll be happy when my mate treats me better. I'll be happy when that raise comes through. But, happiness is a now situation. Happiness happens right now, in the situation that you are in, and, most importantly, it is a choice you are making every moment of every day. I believe that happiness is a conscious choice I make moment by moment, day by day.

The subjective or subconscious mind acts on our words, thoughts and desires. I wanna be... I may be... I hope to be... I wish to be... I try to be... are all tomorrow's wishes, not today's affirmations. Positive statements like: **I am happy, now! I am healthy, now! I am prosperous, now! I am surrounded by loving people, now! I am loved, now!** Thoughts held on a conscious level will eventually imprint on the subjective or subconscious. They will begin to create on the outer what is imprinted on the inner.

REMEMBER: "People are about as happy as they make up their minds to be." (A. Lincoln)

How can you tell what is your present mind-set pattern? Here is an easy test. "HOW ARE YOU?" What is your regular answer? Fine. As well as can be expected. Getting by. I'm feeling poorly. Not very well. What's your automatic answer? Is it time to consciously change your answer? Have you tried, GREAT! I am great!

Our minds are always working. They never take a break. Some kind of thought is going on all the time. Begin today to monitor, to pay attention to your thought. Listen to your automatic responses. They are indicators of what you think about yourself, your life, your health, your relationships. Every part of your world is governed by your thought.

Begin affirming consciously on a regular basis that which you desire to experience. Eventually these positive thoughts will become etched in the mind patterns and will become a reality for you. To change these patterns that have been previously set takes many repetitions of the positive affirmation until they become habitual.

Every so often give yourself the test: "How are you , today?" Listen to the answer. Is that what you desire to experience in your life?

Our minds work all the time and sometimes we have to give them something to work on until we have cleared the negative thoughts that have a habit of returning. Going over the depressed situation again and again only brings you down, so here is a mind game to play. (These thoughts often come when you are driving along or doing some other automatic job.)

ALPHABET AFFIRMATIONS

Beginning with the letter A give thanks for everything that you can think of that are blessings in your life that begin with the letter A. When you have given thanks for all that you can think of go on to the letter B and so on. At the end look at your blessed life with joy and thanksgiving.

IF HAPPINESS IS A CHOICE AND PEOPLE ARE ABOUT AS HAPPY AS THEY CHOOSE TO BE, MAKE UP YOUR MIND TO BE HAPPY!

WHAT'S THE GOOD WORD FOR YOU TODAY?

HAPPINESS

Happiness is a choice
I make each day,
whether to smile
or be sad.

No matter what
the world may show,
It is still my choice
which way to go.

Happiness is a choice
I make each day!

Chapter 10

I'M OK AND I INTEND TO STAY THAT WAY

Are you ready to get off the emotional roller coaster? Does the trauma of depression still have it's hold on you?

Step up to a new world, a new life today, controlled by YOUR mind.

You have learned a great deal about yourself in this drama-trauma you just went through. With the new tools you are learning to use you can overcome any challenge. These tools have held you steady and functioning throughout your experience. Some of them are:

BE TRUE TO YOURSELF. When you are truly doing what is best for you, the whole picture changes, and others are served as well.

KEEP THE FAITH. You have proved over and over that God is supporting you in every way and is so now, this very minute.

STAY ON YOUR PATH. The next step is already prepared for you. Step confidently as if it is so. And it will be. Be watchful, attentive, listening for the sign posts along the way. Stay on course.

KEEP THE VISION. Your vision has not changed. Maybe the location or the situation is different, but your vision, your all-consuming vision, remains awaiting your turning to it.

Perhaps it was the little self that got in the way this time. Resolve to think, act, express and live as your highest self.

Start by planning to level out the emotional responses you give to negative situations. How you act and react when trauma comes your way indicates the depth of the valley.

SET GOALS: Focus your eyes on the higher goals in your life and move your feet towards them. Learn the value of setting goals and reaching them. Start with an easy one and master it like that book you always intended to write or that painting still waiting to be painted. As you become more proficient at setting goals and working toward them, you will discover your emotional pattern will level off.

BE HAPPY: Know that you can be happy no matter what is going on in your world. Start by being happy with yourself. You are a fine, happy person. Let it show to the world that you are happy. SMILE! Other expressions may be fashionable, but put on a smile every day and keep it on.

LISTEN: You inner wisdom never stopped no matter how bad it got. You just stopped listening. So, listen. Your meditation time is the best listening time you will ever have. Do not let a day go by without spending some time in the silence communing with the God Within. It may be revealed that when you stopped meditating regularly, this problem began. Many problem situations can be avoided if you meditate on a regular basis. Start Now!

LEARN WHO YOU ARE: You are a Divine Child of God experiencing a human life. You wield great power. Your thought power creates your world. Begin using your thought power to create the world you desire to experience. How great you are! Your power shapes your life and influences all those around you.

LEARN MENTAL SELF-DISCIPLINE: Hear no evil, see no evil, think no evil, do no evil, and you will discover a whole new world of your making.

YOU CAN DO IT!

Yes, you can! Every time you move toward overcoming depression, God supports you and opens the way.

Learn to trust yourself. In the last trauma you did many right things. You can trust yourself as never before to say the right thing and do the best for yourself and all others.

Your highest self has not been affected by this experience. The innermost part of you is still at peace and is still awaiting your discovery of that great peace. Even in the depth of depression or self-persecution, no one or no thing will judge you. That part of you wherein God resides is always awaiting your turning to it. How wonderful that is.

REMEMBER: When you called, God was there.

TRUST GOD!

REMEMBER: God's will for all of us is to live, laugh, love, learn, listen, be healthy and be happy. God's will is that all eyes be lifted up; to that purpose, we are all striving. As each one of us masters our own depression, we lift another with us until all can joyously proclaim:

I'M FREE! DEPRESSION BE GONE!

Bibliographical Background

Alyce Bartholomew Soden, R.Sc.F. Minister, Practitioner, teacher, author of Prosperity is More than an Attitude, Parenting the Enlightened Child, is the founder of the Light of the Coast Science of Mind Center.

Thirty five years as a successful public school teacher, graduate of Ernest Holmes College 1982 and has been in the pulpit, or assisting ever since.

Also serves as assistant minister to the Walnut Creek Church of Religious Science.

She runs the prestigious Coastal Wedding Service, beautiful weddings, counseling, and the like.

President of Sonoma- Mendocino Coast Soropomist, President of E.S.C.A.P.E.S. Domestic Violence Hot line.

Married June 11,1950 two children, six grand children, Attended & Graduated: Chaffey College, Cal State University, Azusa-Pacific University, Ernest Holmes College.

Enjoys: Research in metaphysics, major interest; birds, composing music, a children's song book, grandchildren, and county living.